Finance Tips & Tricks for First Home Buyers

AUSTRALIAN EDITION

VOLUME 1

First published in 2022

Copyright © Daniel Donnelly

Sherwood Finance Limited
4/129 Kensington High Street
London W8 6BD England

ISBN: 9780645403534 (pbk)

Contents

Introduction

You may remember how you could borrow money from the Bank by taking out a mortgage against one of your properties in the board game Monopoly. If you do not pay the money, you owe the Bank, you can turn over the card and charge the other players rent. You would take out a mortgage against your property as a settlement and get keys from the real estate agent in real life. The scenario from the game is an accurate portrayal of how a mortgage works, but different.

Pre-approval from your chosen lender is essential before you look for the perfect home. Besides knowing whether you qualify for a loan, you will have a clearer picture of how much you can borrow and spend to buy a new home. Do not sign a contract until you are aware of costs associated with buying a home, such as a stamp duty and legal fees. Pre-approval does not guarantee you will be able to get a mortgage on a particular home. Lenders will offer money depending on how much they estimate the home is worth. They may refuse you a loan if they believe you offered too much for the house, or they can offer you a lower loan based on their appraisal.

Topic 1: Lending criteria

The lender looks at several factors to decide whether you are a reliable and upstanding individual with an excellent reputation and, thus, speaking, a safe prospect.

Your ability to service the loan -

Lenders examine whether you can afford to service a particular loan size based on your income and expenses. Their consideration includes how many dependent children you have.

Your assets

Even though your new home is likely to be your biggest asset, a lender will want to know what other assets you have accumulated to understand how your money is being spent. Your assets may include a car, large furniture or home appliances, a share portfolio, and a superannuation account.

Lenders, review your credit history/credit reports

The lender will review your credit obligations and whether you have settled your balances on outstanding bills. If you do not keep on top of your financial comings and goings, your credit score and outcome of the credit application could suffer.

Your employment conditions

To qualify for a loan, you need to have been employed by a single employer for at least three months. Unless you have industry experience several lenders will consider the income.

As part of the application, you will need to show the details of your liabilities, such as payments, outstanding amounts, and the lender that provided the credit. For example, the lender will want to know the limit and include the total repayment amount in the servicing calculator despite even the smallest balance on your credit card or the payment you make. Sometimes, they may even ask that the account be closed before settlement.

Your savings

Your lender will need proof that you have saved at least five per cent of your expected new home purchase price. The policy requires that five per cent of the purchase come from genuine savings accumulated over the last three months. The lender will analyse your savings pattern. Another way to overcome the genuine savings policy is through a rent ledger; for example, you may not have to wait three months to buy housing if you rent and received a gift or inheritance. Many lenders will accept 6- or 12-months' rent ledger if paid on time.

▸ Savings through other means

▸ You have held a term deposit for at least six months.

▸ Investment property or land

▸ Share portfolios or managed funds

What documents to give your lender

You will need similar documentation from lenders if you send your application. They will ask for:

▸ Proof of income

▸ Pay slips from the past two or three months

▸ A score of 100 for identification

▸ Tax returns for two years — self-employed applicants

▸ List of monthly and annual living expenses

▸ Evidence of any other income, such as rental income or Centrelink payments, should be provided

▸ The address where you have lived for the past three years

▸ The last three years' employment history

▸ When you started working at this company

▸ The cost of living each month

Mortgage Insurance

If you can show evidence that you can save five per cent of the expected purchase price of your new home to get a home loan, you will still have to paying mortgage insurance unless you can save twenty per cent plus fees. Lenders' mortgage insurance (or LMI (Lenders Mortgage Insurance) adds thousands of dollars to the loan or deposit, depending on the lender you are speaking with. Lenders' mortgage insurance protects the lender if you cannot repay the loan, and because of the high leveraged lending ratio, the lender might still recover their money.

Despite lenders requiring proof that you can save five per cent of the purchase price, they are not fussy about where the rest of the money comes from. There is no harm in asking friends and family for interest-free loans, although I understand many reading that may not be possible.

2 Banker or Mortgage Broker

Mortgage brokers offer home loans by lenders they are accredited with, known as their panel of lenders. Mortgage brokers handle and administer the loan process through settlement on behalf of the borrower. From January to March 2020, mortgage brokers arranged more than half of new residential mortgages.

Home loan products are available through a mortgage broker. They estimate 16,500 mortgage brokers in Australia, with 80 per cent focused on residential real estate. These operations can range from a one-person, a medium-sized local company to a large national corporation, so your options are endless.

If you have any doubts about the quality of your loan application, mortgage brokers can be invaluable because they understand how lenders assess loan applications. In addition, they will know a specific lender that increases the chances of approval, and they may realise policy niches that play into why you would choose one lender over another.

The extra stress of resubmitting your application to another lender and waiting for the credit assessor to review your file will affect your credit history. When you apply with multiple lenders for the same purpose, so you will want to avoid this scenario. A mortgage broker who places your application with a lender receives an upfront commission when settlement occurs, and often ongoing commissions can begin up to a month after sale.

The amount of bank branches in Australia has decreased because of the rise of mortgage brokers. Banks still offer a lot of value. They are accessible to an array of individuals looking to borrow money. Getting an idea of the terms and conditions with your current bank (where your income is credited) is wise before speaking with a mortgage broker. The benefits of contacting the banks may vary by the level of service and cost of their mortgage loans. The internet can be beneficial in saving time when making comparison searches (you may even find a comparison site that will do the arduous work for you).

3 Lenders

The leading four

The four major banks, ANZ (Australasian and New Zealand) Commonwealth Bank of Australia (CBA), National Australia Bank (NAB), and Westpac Banking Corporation (WBC). still led most of the mortgages in Australia, with around 80 per cent of the loans approved between them. In addition, online banking, 24/7 telephone support and integrated bank packages, such as transaction offset accounts, credit cards and insurance, are available to customers. The not-so-good news is that there are many scandals and reports of their record-breaking profits that were made at the customer's expense on the information over the years.

The second tier has Bank West, Bendigo, and Adelaide Bank, which offer integrated banking packages, more individualised services, and greater flexibility. Non-bank lenders became the norm because of the deregulation of the banking system in the 1980s. Their first and most significant success came from Aussie home loans, which arrived just in time to ride the first big anti-bank wave of the 1990s and undercut banks' interest rates.

Case Study

Self employed

Property details

At the southern coastal area of New South Wales, detached residential house was ideal for a first home buyer.

What the client wanted

the client had been to his current bank, but they refused finance because after averaging his earlier two years financials it failed servicing.

Key details

When assessing servicing, most lenders ask for the earlier two year's financials, which sometimes can reduce the income available for servicing the loan. But we were aware of a lending policy whereby they took only the last years financials.

The result

The outcome was great because we got the file approved from a major lender, conditions were standard valuation and final assessment. Our client went onto settle on that property.

Building societies and credit unions

There is a significant difference between banks, building societies, and credit unions. On the one hand, they get their money from traditional lenders, and on the other, they get it from non-traditional lenders. Unlike conventional lenders, non-bank lenders source their funding from international capital markets (international investors seeking returns on secure Australian mortgages at fixed interest rates). During the recent monetary crisis, these lenders have had difficulty offering lending terms to property buyers in Australia. As a result, this part of the market has seen significant changes and takeovers, while other lending institutions have deserted the market altogether.

Besides offering low rates and often no ongoing fees, many credit unions offer comprehensive banking services. Until the mid-1980s, the building societies and credit unions offered loans when the banks refused. These institutions charged higher interest rates to cover the more significant risks with mortgages, but they were less efficient overall. These building societies and credit unions have provided loans to their members as not-for-profit institutions.

Home loan offers may still be available from the original mortgage lenders. Creating and providing customised service distinguishes most of today's building societies and credit unions from their banking competitors. the operators are state-wide or national in scope, but most are in a limited of states and regions. Because of the power of the internet, mortgages are more accessible than ever, and many building societies and credit unions are competing online for certain types of consumers.

Non-conforming Lenders

Among the most recent innovations in mainstream lending is the emergence of non-conforming lenders. In the late 1990s when a vacuum in the middle market arose, filling the gap between traditional lenders and private lenders who lend on the property as a last resort sometimes.

In these instances, the former credit would have caused a default on your credit report because of your bad debts, unpaid loans, late repayments or bill payments, or bankruptcy history. As a result, depending on your earlier conduct, they might decline your application for a mortgage or any other credit.

Sometimes you can appeal a lender's decision by explaining how the default occurred. We can refer you two professionals who specialise in dealing with lenders on your behalf to remove the default. the lenders consider credit-impaired applications on a case-by-case basis. Specialised lenders, rather than regular banks, give these home loans. They have stricter lending criteria and do not have the same fees as traditional home loans.

They set individual mortgage rates for their borrowers, non-confirming lenders use a method known as risk-based pricing. These lenders play a crucial role in the Australian lending market in that they charge customers an interest rate that reflects the risk they pose of defaulting on the mortgage. They target borrowers who, because of a genuine temporary mishap, find they cannot get home loans from mainstream lenders.

Such customers include poor credit records, self-employed people, and people with irregular income streams, such as consultants and freelancers. Non-confirming loans have high-interest rates at first and can be refinanced into mainstream loans with reduced interest rates.

Case study

Property details

The client was seeking to purchase a property in the southern coastal areas of Queensland.

What did the client want?

After meeting a representative from his bank, they informed the client that they would use his last two years' financials for servicing and not his current income. so, the client needed a lender to consider his current YTD (Year to date) income rather than his earlier year's income.

What did we do?

We engaged a non-conforming lender which enabled his accountant to verify YTD income to support the application.

Key points

Mortgage insurance companies do not support low documentation applications; so, 20 per cent plus government fees are required.

The results

They approved finance; the client was pleased with the outcome.

Mortgage managers

A mortgage manager acts as an intermediary between a non-bank lender and a borrower. Rather than getting deposits from customers, they get their funds from investors and mortgage trusts. A mortgage originator can recommend the services of a mortgage manager to take care of the loan.

4 Products

The bank has been lending people money to buy properties for hundreds of years. To make their money back, they charge an additional amount on top of the mortgage from the day of settlement. This extra money is known as interest and added to the loan you take out, but not hidden or added without warning. You will get a statement notifying you of the amount owed and how much paid so far. If you do not keep up with your payments, your lender will call you and chase you up, and even charge a fee. This will happen between 15 to 30 days after receiving a statement. The lender may increase interest to the default charges listed in the loan agreement.

People often confuse mortgages with home loans, but the mortgage part shows through a written contract the ownership that the lender has over your home as security for the loan, as displayed because the lender holds the title to your home until you pay off the rest of the loan.

Many people find the notion that their lender owns a majority share of their home to be depressing, and their primary aim in life is to pay off their mortgage as quickly as possible. But you can think of paying off a mortgage just like paying an internet or phone bill. It is better to have a mortgage than pay rent because although the rent may increase, the repayments of the loan over time will decrease, and the house's value will increase. Not only that, but the property will be yours, with no one else staking a claim on if anything were to go wrong. The property you own, and love will never be yours when you rent.

Home loans are one of the most significant sources of income for lenders. But, throughout your mortgage, you may end up paying as much in interest as you borrowed, not to mention the upfront and ongoing fees levied by the lender to cover administration and other loan servicing costs. Lenders need to avoid creating unmanageable debt by taking on borrowers who might not pay back the loan. Lenders have no choice of foreclosing on your home if you default on your payments. but lenders are inclined to avoid this arduous and often expensive step.

Even though a mortgage involves a lot of cash, your lender's money is at risk rather than yours. Because of this arrangement, if the lending company collapses, your equity is unaffected. As a result, it is likely that another lending company will take over a lender's loan book, which is an asset for them and a bonus for you eventually.

Credit can be helpful to many ways, but it comes risks. The loan you borrow must be repaid, with a regular payment schedule. Those who use credit and allow their debt to spiral out of control will head into financial difficulty. Higher interest will be charged, the amount that you owe could exceed your ability to pay. if unpaid could result in the loss of the house. Therefore, if you cannot make your payments, you may experience a heavy price. You can ruin your reputation as a borrower if you cannot repay loans. using too much credit can lead to problems in families and relationships. The good news is most people manage the mortgage responsibly and go onto spend their retirement debt free or even buy other properties.

Case study

Casual employment

Property Details

An apartment in Melbourne south. The property was ideal for the client, proximity to her work and community.

What did the client want?

The client had been to their current lender, but because of their length of casual employment; the lender refused finance but encouraged to reapply in six months. But the client did not want to miss the property.

Key details

When assessing casual income, there is several lenders that take a different approach.

The result

Our experience resulted in approval for the client, and they settled way before the other lender encouraged them to reapply.

Guarantor mortgages

Guarantees may be provided by individuals, companies, or partnerships. We sometimes refer them to as sureties. When taking guarantors, a lender must exercise great caution. In one sense, it wants to be certain that it takes all legal measures to make sure the guarantor pays, in another words, it does not want to take any risks. They must prevent the guarantor from absolving themselves of responsibility, the lenders will want to guard against the guarantor appealing the guarantee's validity, claiming that they did not explain the terms, or that they were under undue pressure to sign. An independent legal opinion is required every prospective guarantor before acting. What you need to know about guarantees If the borrower defaults on repayment, the lender can enforce them from the guarantee. If a guarantor asks for information, unless they are specific, the borrower is under no obligation to show it.

As the prices of properties rise, many first-time buyers find it hard to get a mortgage large enough to purchase a property. It is because they cannot reach the required minimum deposit. To solve this issue, the lenders have introduced guarantor mortgages, which operate on the same principles as any ordinary guarantor-backed mortgage however, they marketed it as a specific product. Mortgages are the same as any other loan mortgage product, it may offer fixed or variable rates in line with standard products, and principal and interest repayment or interest-only options.

For security, lenders will take charge of the guarantor's property to prove the guarantor can pay both their own obligations on the guarantor's mortgage. A guarantor is required, as with many loan guarantees, to seek independent legal advice to ensure that they understand what they are signing up for. Most guarantor mortgages are short term because once the lending leverage reduces to eighty percent of the property value, the guarantor property can be released.

Parents offer guarantees for their children's borrowing on behalf of themselves as guarantors. Companies often ask for director guarantees to help secure loans made to the company, because a loan is enforceable only against the company, not its shareholders, and not against its directors. Undertaking to guarantee the loan ensures that the directors are supportive of the company and confirming it meets its obligations. If the borrower will not or cannot repay the loan, the lender assumes responsibility.

A guarantor does not own the property they are guaranteeing a mortgage on and has no right to inspect mortgage documents or be informed of missed mortgage repayments. Often, a problem does not come to the guarantor's attention until the lender insists on payment. If the mortgage holder requests a further advance or an extension of the term, the guarantor must be informed, and can refuse consent. Lenders will not release guarantors unless they feel the borrower can manage the mortgage without posing a risk to them.

Case Study

Property details

The house on the gold coast was not your standard purchase for a first-time buyer.

What did the client want?

Because of the amount of mortgage insurance charged, it deterred the client from multiple lenders offer of finance.

Key details

When the loan amount exceeds eighty percent of the property value, its standard across the lenders to charge an insurance premium. There is an alternative by arranging another security to secure part of the loan, which then reduces the loan amount on that property being purchased.

The result

The client asked his parents, and they offered their investment property to secure the amount to avoid the mortgage insurance premium. So, the finance went ahead without any mortgage insurance paid.

Standard Variable Rate

Standard variable rates are often the first interest rates mentioned when speaking with lenders about home loans and their features and functions. Most banking institutions offer this under a different name. Still, full-service loans can be a good fit for most borrowers, making the lending decision smoother and quicker for those with no unusual requirements or issues. When discussing rising or falling mortgage interest rates, media outlets cite this figure, known as the SVR. SVRs are the highest interest rate charged to mortgage customers, but they may include other products, which may be helpful. Offset accounts, redraw accounts and fee-free general banking are notable examples.

Despite being the most often quoted rate, few customers pay it. Most banks discount the offered interest rate from the loan to value ratio, especially for property buyers who have a higher-than-average loan balance.

Discount variable rates.

Discount variable rates for no-frills mortgages are advertised lower than standard variable rates. but these will not always offer access to products such as offset accounts, redraw accounts and fee-free banking.

With low-value properties, these low ever rate products may be an excellent choice for starters. Even if you buy a more expensive first property, the Bank may offer you the extra features with a standard rate instead of an interest rate associated with a discounted mortgage.

Fixed or Variable

Each has its pros and cons, and in most cases, with real estate investment, one of the most important considerations is whether a fixed or variable rate will be ideal for your needs.

Many circumstances will help an investor decide on a variable rate loan, such as handling potential interest rates rises. Long-term variable rates work out more economically, but it's always best to consider both options before deciding.

If you want more certainty apply for a fixed rate. A fixed rate will allow you to fil your repayments into your budget without having to worry about any interest fluctuations.

While most lenders have a buffer and review your living expenses before offering finance. When the interest rate increases, the property owners might struggle to meet the requirements of their higher monthly repayments.

When considering variable rate loans, you may make unlimited contributions to the mortgage. In contrast, fixed-rate repayments are capped per annum, and how much varies with the lender.

The offset Account

An offset account, not available with all loans, may prove to be a valuable extra string in your bow. Offset accounts give the borrower the freedom to deposit and save money, as well if linked to your mortgage loan account, it offsets the interest charged on the balance of the loan amount.

For example, with a mortgage loan balance of $500,000 and $40,000 sitting in the offset account over the month, interest is calculated on a loan balance of $460,00 because of the $40,000 sitting in the offset account. Keep in mind the lender charges interest daily on the balance of the loan account, so money going in and out of the offset account will affect the amount of interest saved.

There is only one offset account with a loan package, so attach the offset account to the home loan mortgage to offset the interest charged. There is no benefit in attaching an offset account to an investment property loan, as all the interest charged is tax deductible.

Interest-only loans

When buying a property to occupy you need a good explanation for why you are applying for interest-only loans. Satisfactory reasons do exist, but it is better to speak with us before choosing that lender, as we can suggest a lender that is opened to only offering interest on loans. A downside of interest-only loans is that the balance owed does not decrease with the property's value, so if the property's value drops, you might need to borrow more money to cover the difference or end up with negative equity.

Case Study

Discharged bankrupt

Property details

On the inner eastern suburbs of Adelaide. the townhouse was located for client workplaces and children's schools.

What did the client want?

In the past the clients had experienced hard financial times from a family emergency. As a result, they went into bankruptcy and after being discharged, they contacted our team to explore their options.

Difficulties along the way

The discharged bankruptcy could be overcome, but the deposit available was the least and they also needed a lender that would capitalise the mortgage insurance premium above the most lenders requirements.

Key details

We knew from the get-go that the mainstream lenders would not consider the application, so we resorted to our non-conforming lenders.

The result

After explaining how the financial hardship occurred, they approved the finance. The outcome was ideal.

5 Working with property sector professionals.

Real estate agent

Rather than representing the buyer, real estate agents represent the seller (who is more commonly known as the vendor). The good ones are responsive, transparent and they have all the answers to the buyer's questions. Many of them work under the assumption that buyers become sellers and will want to stay on your good side while acting in the vendor's best interests. The local real estate institute of Australia can give you information about the real estate agent you are dealing with. First, conduct an internet search to find the local REIA contact details, as the rules and regulations vary from state to state. When you see an ideal property in a newspaper or on a website. You should contact the agent handling it for more information, schedule an inspection before making an offer.

The first and most important thing to remember when working with a real estate agent they must look out for the seller's best interests. Most real estate agents make most of their income from commissions negotiated with the seller before listing a property. A real estate agent earns a commission based on the sale price of the property, and sometimes the commission may be scaled so they have an added incentive for the sale price to be higher.

At first, remember that the real estate agent that you are dealing with is not your friend. They are skilled at connecting with their clients, making you believe they are working to find you a property that you will be happy with. Still, their legal duty (and often financial interest) is to represent the seller and increase the sale price as much as possible. This does not mean that they are bad people deep down, just that they are good at their jobs; they can still give great insight into the local market and valuable information about the entire process.

At the heart of it, the selling agent's goal is to generate the most interest and promote competition between as many buyers as possible to achieve the highest price. This goal motivates the agent, but not every property sells. This means that, there may be a window of opportunity for the savvy home buyer when an agent's motives change as the property sits on the market for months.

Buyer's Agents

Buyers' agents are often former selling agents. As a result, your buyer's agent may give you access to properties that have not yet been advertised, silent listings and much more, depending on their network and experience.

They will check for flaws within a particular property, in terms of suitability. By removing the emotional and stressful elements of house-hunting from the process, you may take the stress out of everything. Then, the agent will come back to you with a list of properties that may meet your needs after telling them what you are looking for, how much you will spend and where you want to buy.

Because most buyer's agents have current knowledge of the market, they are aware of any changes in sentiment and the recent sales of comparable properties. When you are considering hiring a buyer's agent, consider the following three ways buyers can charge for their services:

▸ A flat fee for the service

▸ Fees based on your budgeted purchase price

▸ Fees based on the actual purchase price

A buyer's agent may charge a retainer (or an engagement) fee of several hundred dollars upfront. In addition, they may charge you further success fees in any of the three ways described above when they find and purchase a property on your behalf.

Conveyancers or Solicitors

Conveyancing, in legal terms, refers to transferring the real estate ownership. Depending on the state you live in, either a solicitor or a specialist conveyancing firm should be able to handle the transfer. There are many boxes to be ticked, forms to be filled out, and government agencies to contact regarding property transfer.

Prior to attending an auction, you need to hire a conveyancer who will inspect the property for title issues and review pre-sale documents. If you are not sure who to contact, reach out to us, and we will refer you to a trustworthy professional.

First Homeowner Grants

State and federal governments offer several thousand dollars to aid first-time buyers. In addition, First-home-owner grants were introduced in 2000 to help families, couples, and individuals get on the property ladder, as they understood the ongoing difficulties for many to do so. The acronym FHOGs (First Homeowner s Grants) are paid by each state and territory government and come with rules that can change.

First home buyers, for example, may be eligible for a first home buyer bonus and rebate to assist with the cost of stamp duty (a state tax on the purchase price of a property). In most states and territories, concessions on stamp duty rates are available on property purchases to a certain amount. In addition, first-time homeowners receive grants based on their state. As these grants are subject to change and can change over time, so it is best to check with your broker or do a search online to make sure how much funds are available at the time of settlement.

For current information on the grants available you can search online or phone the following department.

New South Wales

https://www.revenue.nsw.gov.au/grants-schemes/
first-home-buyer/new-homes

South Australia

https://www.revenuesa.sa.gov.au/FHOG

Tasmania

https://www.sro.tas.gov.au/first-home-owner

Western Australia

First home owner grant (FHOG) (www.wa.gov.au)

Victoria

First Home Owner | State Revenue Office (sro.vic.gov.
au)

Queensland

Queensland First Home Owners' Grant | Homes and
housing | Queensland Government (www.qld.gov.au)

Australian capital territory

First Home Owner Grant | ACT Revenue Office
- Website

Northern Territory

https://treasury.nt.gov.au/

6 Deciding where to buy

You will have an easier time searching for real estate once you know the type of property you want. Depending on your preferences, the house-hunting process could take weeks or even months. Finding the perfect home for a reasonable price can become a full-time obsession for people, and many have spent a year searching for a house to buy.

You need to know what you want, where to look and be organised to maximise your chances of finding the right property, regardless of whether you are an obsessive or a practical who prefers to get things done. This chapter explains the different methods and ways to search for a property that can simplify the process.

Make notes of the essential features you hope to find in a property and the property you are looking for before you begin your first search. You can use a checklist of must-haves and must not have to give you a more realistic view of your preferences. A preliminary benchmark is beneficial if you are looking for real estate with others. Benchmarks are a valuable tool for guiding your search strategy and helping you narrow down the number of properties you need to consider. You will change and refine the criteria during your search, but you will at least have something to begin with.

By this time, you should have received pre-approval for a home loan amount before you search for a home. By knowing how much you can borrow, you will have a clearer picture of how much you can spend on your new home, which will make it easier for you to come to a well-informed decision when browsing the real estate market.

Try to find every source of information about properties for sale to maximise your chances of finding the home that best suits your needs. You should not rely only on the internet, as convenient as it may be, nor on referrals from your chosen real estate agent. Instead, search and open-mindedly, and you might find a hidden gem and be prepared miss to out on the property you have set your heart on. Having a philosophical approach to home searching will make sure that you do not end up in despair.

Internet searches are the most current way to find real estate. The internet has transformed how property is bought and sold. Over the past decade, and, you have already visited significant sites such as property.com.au or domain.com.au before reading this book. You can find homes for sale, rent, and share on these sites, as well as articles on home improvements, renovations and even the current state and trends of the property market.

There are many ways to search for properties via the web, including suburb, price, and the number of bedrooms. These websites let you further filter their results by desirable local amenities, schools, parks, entertainment and transport, and specific property features such as solar panels and air conditioning. Both websites allow you to make shortlists of properties you are interested in so that you can receive emails with properties matching your criteria. Keeping track of what is happening to a particular property can be done via these websites' software; you will need is to visit the correct section on the one you are using. If the property has sold, you will be notified here too, and you may even find auctioned properties that are available for private sale, showing that the vendors are now accepting offers.

All of this makes these types of property-finding websites well worth your time. Having access to the information you could want could spell the difference between you finding your dream home in next to no time and sitting out in the cold waiting for something to come up.

Though you may have a suburb in mind, why not look at one or two suburbs further afield if the ideal one is out of your price range? You are not limited to just one option, and you might find the perfect property for in a short time.

First-time homeowners have always had to embark on new ventures, and if you choose your suburb, it can be an excellent investment. Over time, the suburbs have become popular. For example, those who bought in Brunswick in Melbourne or Newtown in Sydney ten years ago enjoy a fantastic way of life, as the suburbs have grown. These areas have become more attractive, with intriguing shops and cafes and better facilities increasing the economic climate.

> You may wish to look at districts that are underdeveloped or construction sites taking place or look at new shops and cafes that have appeared. Keep in mind that excellent shopping facilities, public transportation and freeways are likely to keep their value.

House and land packages

Every month, new housing estates are under construction around the edges of Australian cities. These developments offer terms that do not need you to put down a full deposit to get a new home with the extras for a lot less than the price of equivalent properties in the city centre. Often, these estates are full of children and have facilities that cater to the needs of young families, so they can be ideal for those planning to start one. Besides providing access to the countryside and fresh air, these areas often offer opportunities for outdoor activities. There are grants available to first-time homeowners in most states in Australia, which can reduce the deposit amount required.

The best investment decision may not always be to buy a house and land package. It costs more to buy properties in the inner city and on the waterfront since the rarity value of the land determines the value. In addition, as the inner city cannot expand and water frontages are finite, outer suburban housing estates are replicable, complicating resale.

Instead of buying a house and land package from a project builder, you could build your own home to suit your specific needs. Suppose this is the route you want to take. In that case, hire an architect to design your home according to your specifications and use a project manager to instigate and oversee construction, coordinating the builders and tradespeople from start to finish.

Your dream home can be designed by you, with the help of a tradesperson, if necessary, and built by you and a general contractor.

Apartments

The high-rise apartment lifestyle has only become a choice for Australians and immigrants outside of Sydney and Melbourne. Most Australians are used to having a backyard to play cricket or entertain guests, but urban areas are now being developed with multi-unit, high-rise buildings. Besides the potential for stunning views, many newer developments come furnished with modern conveniences. Several of them offer amenities such as swimming pools, fitness centres and cafes, which are besides concierge and security services. First home buyers might find buying an apartment more affordable, given that housing prices in most capital cities in Australia are unaffordable.

You should not expect your purchases to be wise

investments. There is a problem with high-rise apartments, too, much like outer suburban housing estates; they are in abundant supply, and another newer and fancier building nearby may limit capital gains. but there are great government incentives for purchasing inner-city apartments in the of the larger cities.

Regional

They reported people leaving the city for coastal and rural areas to live a more relaxed lifestyle. Among the benefits are the fresh air, the animals, the beautiful scenery, and the locals' friendliness. It is a growing trend in this area, especially among retirees and those able to work from home.

Buying off the plan

There are many similarities between buying a unit or apartment off the plan (otherwise known as pre-construction) and having a house built for you based on the options available by viewing a related show-home. An apartment of this is in a building that has not been built yet. It is not just the apartment itself but the quality and facilities of the structure, which determines how happy you will live there. Stamp duty savings are available in several states. If you plan to live in a multi-level apartment, you have less control over how designed and constructed than if you are building a home for you. It may be worthwhile to gather as much information as possible on the planned facilities and aesthetics of the overall build before deciding on the unit you may buy within it.

Before purchasing any real estate It's recommended to arrange a building inspector.

7 Auction or Private treaty

A good auction can be exciting, whether it is in-house or even held on a suburban street. It can become so intense that the bids can sometimes go beyond what was expected because of popular demand. The aim of an auction is to create a large, exciting atmosphere for a sale while also providing bidders and sellers with transparency.

When considering bidding at an auction, it is essential that you first set yourself a budget (and a firm limit) before consulting your solicitor or accountant. If you have any enquiries, contact our team.

If an auction does not meet the vendor's expectations and the last bid is declared to be insufficient by the vendor, the property will often be passed on to the highest bidder or will be reverted to a private treaty sale. The same goes for other situations, too, like if there are no genuine bidders.

If there are several under-bidders, the sale will be passed in, and the highest bidder will have a private conversation about the vendor's reserve level. Agents are likely to tell everyone involved that there is still a chance to take the property for a higher bid, although the first bidder is given the first right of refusal. If they are not satisfied with the reserve price, the agents can continue negotiations with under-bidders.

Auction or private treaty often comes down to producing the best results. In some circumstances, auctions can seem like the best solution, where several investors will be prepared to outdo each other to get the property regardless of the extra money they are investing.

Many homes are sold by private treaties in Australia. Vendors (sellers) decide the price at which they market their properties for sale under this process. If the buyer is not happy with the price, they begin negotiations by offering a lower one. building inspection.

Negotiation is a natural part of buying or selling a property by private treaty. To get the highest price, a seller often looks for a private treaty sale to work like a slow-motion auction, i.e., offers come in and move back and forth between the seller and purchaser. Rather than taking place during a one half-hour auction with other bidders in front of the property, this may take place over hours, and sometimes days, weeks, or even months.

A seller's agent receives the offer. When a vendor agrees to a request, they will ask the agent to accept it, and contracts are then written and exchanged. A private treaty can seem less stressful and more straightforward compared to an auction sale or purchase. keep in mind that a private treaty requires more negotiation skills from the seller's agent.

Some states need you make an offer in writing, often by filling out a form and signing it. For example, you can put in a verbal offer in New South Wales, Queensland, Victoria, and the Northern Territory and the ACT (Australian Capital Territory), if they are in writing offers are taken more seriously.

We suggest following the procedure set out in your state or territory. If the vendor agrees to your offer and any conditions you set, you both sign and exchange the contract document, making the agreement binding. but consider the following explanations as a guide because local governments and buyers often scrutinise the auction process, and the process could change.

Victoria

Auction

At the start of the auction, there is no requirement to register your intent to bid, unless a condition imposed by the real estate agency. Only the auctioneer may make a vendor bid, and they must announce a 'vendor bid.' If a co-owner intends to bid, the auctioneer must disclose this at the commencement of the auction Bidders can ask during the auction if the property is 'on the market.' Dummy bids are prohibited by law. For mortgagee sales, Deceased estates or Family Law Matters, the property must go to auction; therefore, the agent cannot convey offers prior to the auction date.

Private treaty

Unless instructed otherwise all offers must be in writing by the vendor. Besides written submissions, buyers can also make verbal offers, submit a completed contract of sale, and offer a deposit. After the vendor accepts your offer, it becomes binding only when you and the vendor exchange contracts, and a deposit (10%) is accounted for

Tasmania

Auction

Have your finance and deposit ready on the day is essential. Vendors may bid up to the reserve price, and the auctioneer must state vendor bids to potential buyers assembled at the auction. If the offers do not reach the reserve, you may negotiate with the vendor afterwards and settle on a negotiated price. On the day contracts of Sale are signed and exchanged. Dummy bidding is prohibited.

Private treaty

To make an offer, buyers should use the law society contract of sale provided by their agent. If you wish, you can ask your attorney or conveyancer to prepare the offer document for you. The agent must pass on all offers but may not if the request is below the vendor's stipulated amount. They do not require sellers to show known defects with the property. A cooling-off period of three days. But if both parties choose not to use it, no cooling-off period applies. Once the contract of sale is signed by both parties and exchanged, finance proceeds

New South Wales

Auction

To take part or bid at a residential auction, potential buyers must register by showing identification and will be given a bidder's number. The auctioneer oversees the bidding process. The vendor sets the reserve price before the auction and is entitled to one vendor bid. If they do not meet the reserve price, the highest bidder is asked to negotiate with the sales agent. Unless agreed before the auction, a ten per cent deposit is required at the fall of the hammer. Ensure finances are ready as contracts will be exchanged on the day. Dummy bids are illegal.

Private treaty

Offers can be verbal or in writing. Although making a formal offer, the vendor is more likely to accept. When the vendor accepts your request, a five-day cooling-off period begins. The buyers and sellers are not bound until signed contracts are exchanged. Then titles are prepared, loan documentation is returned signed, and settlement can be completed. This takes between 30 two 90 days The buyer is required to pay a deposit.

Australian Capital Territory

Auction

You must register to bid by providing the real estate agent at the auction with proof of your identity, and a bidder's number will be assigned to you. The agent can make one vendor bid on behalf of the vendor and must be stated as a vendor bid. The highest bidder must exceed the reserve price set before the auction begins. If the reserve is not met, the highest bidder will negotiate with the sales agent. The highest bidder will have to sign contracts and pay the agreed deposit on the day. Finance must be in place to meet settlement under absolute terms, and 'dummy bidding' is prohibited.

Private treaty

Agents must notify the vendor of all offers and must be in writing. The advertised price must be similar and close to what the seller will accept. The seller can receive offers from other interested parties until contracts are exchanged. After accepting the offer, the sales agent will send the contract and offer documentation to the buyer's solicitor. Once the buyer and seller have both signed and exchanged the contract, it becomes binding. The five-day cooling-off period can only be waived or amended with signed approval from the vendor.

Western Australia

Auction

Auctions are not as common in Western Australia as in other states. The auctioneer starts by detailing the benefits of the property and any relevant information and restrictions on the title. In addition, the required deposit to be paid must be disclosed before commencing. The auctioneer then calls for or announces an opening bid, below the reserve price. Offers from vendors are permitted. It must be specified in the auction form whether the seller will make bids and how many. On the fall of the hammer, the agreed deposit will be paid. Contracts exchanged on the day. Dummy bids are illegal.

Private treaty

If you suggest making an offer, buyers must fill out and sign an offer and acceptance contract (O & A). The agent will prepare either of the two forms, Contract for Sale of Land and General Conditions or the Strata Title, and the agent will present the offer to the vendor. The vendor may either accept or counter the offer by amending the O & A or reject it, and the agent must inform the purchaser. Once the offer is accepted, the settlement must occur within the agreed timeframe

Queensland

Auction

Before the auction begins, you must register with the auctioneer. A number paddle is provided. Until the reserve price, vendor bids can be accepted, provided the auctioneer announces them in the conditions of sale at the beginning of the auction. Auctioneers cannot engage in dummy bidding or take false bids. After the auction, contracts are signed, and a five to ten per cent deposit is paid

Private treaty

Agents can list prices over the least amount the vendor will accept. Agents are prohibited from listing below the vendors' minimum price, often considered bait advertising, which is an offence. Verbal offers can be made, and all written offers must be sent to the vendor. When your offer is accepted, the agent must give you a contract of sale, accompanied by a warning statement. The purchaser will need to pay a deposit after the five-day cooling-off period. This takes between 30 - 90 days for settlement

South Australia

Auction

You must register by providing your identification to the agent conducting the sale. For someone else to bid on your behalf, you will need to give proof of your identity plus a signed authorisation letter. A reserve price is set, in writing, before the auction. You should know the vendor is entitled to three bids. The vendor bids must not exceed the reserve price. The auctioneer must announce each such bid as a 'vendor bid'. If reported throughout the auction, it shows that the vendor's reserve price is not reached. If you are the highest bidder and the reserve price is not met, you can negotiate. At the fall of the hammer, if you are the successful bidder a ten per cent deposit is required. It would be best if you had your finance ready because they exchange contracts on the day. Dummy bids are not allowed.

Private treaty

All offers must be in writing that discloses the seller's name, contact information, the price, the settlement date, and any other conditions. Each submission can include a date by which the offer lapses. Before a vendor accepts an offer, the agent must make sure the vendor has received all written offers. Requests are often subject to building inspection and loan approval or any other conditions by the purchaser or vendor. Both parties must sign a contract of sale before the offer is binding. To complete the settlement, it can take from 30 to 90 days.

Northern Territory

Auction

On the day, the auctioneer will detail the terms and conditions of the auction process and then call for bids on the property. All bidders must register by showing identification. The Auctioneers must not engage in conduct that is fraudulent or misleading. Dummy bids are prohibited. Before the auction, the vendor will set a 'reserve price', and the property will be passed in unless the bidding reaches that point. An auctioneer will often advise the attendees that the property is 'on the market', showing it has passed the reserve price and will be sold to the highest bidder. If the reserve is not met, bidders are invited to negotiate to purchase the property with the selling agent. As usual, make sure that finance is ready to meet the agreed settlement date

Private treaty

An offer on a property should be on a formal contract, although buyers can make verbal offers, and all offers must be sent to the vendor. The vendor is not bound to accept your submission until the contract of sale are exchanged. At the time of the exchange, the purchaser is required to pay a deposit. The settlement process can take from 30 to 90 days.

Settling on your property

In legal and financial coordination, settlement is when can be completed. Settlement of course also means you can move into your home.

When the contract is exchanged with the vendor on the date specified in the contract of sale, all parties must perform the required legal work. You will also need to schedule for the lender to arrange funding to be available for settlement.

The conveyancer or solicitor arranges for you to sign a document confirming the ownership transfer at least a week before the settlement date. It may be wise to note that your conveyancer or solicitor will notify you a few days before settlement of the exact date and time of the sale going through, and the required funds to provide for settlement to go ahead. Once this is complete, you will collect your keys and move on in and now you are the proud owner of a home!

Some tips. Before settlement ask for inspection to make sure all furniture from the property has been removed. Also make sure there are no surprises, such as broken windows or discarded appliances (even items like brand-new dishwashers can pose issues when buying/selling property). Items left in the property and included in the sale must be documented in the Sale Contract.

8 Key legal concepts

Understanding the basics of a contract

The purchase contract, which is referred to as the contract of sale, is the most critical document in any real estate transaction. When you have found a property you like, get the seller's agreement, and have your solicitor/ conveyancer check it for irregularities before you make an offer.

In real estate, a contract is an agreement between two or more people regarding exchanging property. Unlike ordinary contracts, these contracts contain enforceable promises that must be fulfilled. But they are governed by the basics of contract law.

The parties must agree on how the contract will be interpreted, understood, and enforced — and there must be a consideration (money) passed between them. Also, there must be an intention of both parties to be bound by the contract. If it contains the elements that make it enforceable, such a contract is valid. The terms may sound technical, but you need to be familiar with them.

Ownership

Getting the proper ownership structure is essential, as it could save you thousands. The correct answer to your situation can depend on a variety of factors. So, it is best to talk with an expert to improve your understanding of the options, and here are two major structures to consider: Joint ownership (partner, friend, family member, etc.)

In most instances, joint ownership will have similar implications to individual ownership, aside from the fact that you need to consider the amount of holding between partners and whether you would prefer joint tenants or tenants in common.

They do not divide the property with joint tenants, and each owner has one hundred per cent ownership over it. Should one of the joint owners die, the other takes legal ownership of the property. The process is automatic and cannot be overridden by any other means, for example, a will or the laws of intestacy.

With tenants in common, both owners are considered a single entity and are trustees of the land, although each is still the owner of an agreed interest in the property's equity (which is defined by the owners). If one dies, their share goes to whoever may inherit based on their will or the law of intestacy.

It is important to understand that the words 'tenant' and 'tenancy' do not involve renting the property but refer to the joint ownership of an asset (of any form, not just property). These terms apply to loans (such as mortgages), and with joint tenants, all borrowers will be responsible for the total debt. Tenants in common are liable for their part of the debt. banks and other lenders will encourage borrowers to get joint mortgages written on a joint tenancy basis.

Wills

As your wealth and assets increase over time, it can become vital for you to write and complete a will. It is common for rewritten wills as circumstances change. As most people know, a will is a declaration of how you want your assets distributed, as well as other matters. For a will to be valid, it must follow these crucial rules.

▸ It must be in writing

▸ Executed correctly in most cases with a lawyer

▸ Executor appointed

If someone dies without a will, they have died intestate, including those who made an invalid will. There is provision for distributing assets, but not all.

Conveyancing

In theory, you do not need a solicitor to handle the legal formalities in a property buy or sell, but no lender will issue a mortgage unless an attorney handles the legal formalities. So, while most buyers use a licensed conveyancer, a solicitor is appointed in most cases. A licensed conveyancer must have qualifications and be certified to practise and is limited to dealing with real estate-related matters, unlike a solicitor.

PEXA's world-first digital settlements have revolutionised the way properties have been exchanged in Australia. Over 20,000 homes a week are settled for families through faster access to the proceeds of a sale and near real-time tracking. Most settlements occur online nowadays, and before you collect the keys from your agent, the conveyancing process must be completed.

The term conveyancing refers to the transferral of a property. Depends on the state in Australia you are in, you will need to choose either a solicitor or a specialist firm to take care of the conveyance. Specialist conveyancers are not lawyers, but they can often care for the legal necessities.

You should always have a specialist review the contract before attending an auction. They will research any property title issues and review the pre-sale document. but, if you are not sure how to find one, contact us, and we will help you find a trustworthy professional.

Debt and insolvency problems

During insolvency, a person's liabilities exceed their assets, and the borrower cannot meet their financial obligations within a reasonable amount of time. insolvency accountants act on behalf of the client and work with the debtors and creditors. As a result, the insolvency accountant will decide what remaining assets can be distributed to creditors after all deductions have been made, such as the Australian Tax office (tax debt), legal fees, and accounting fees.

Powers of Attorney: What are they?

If an individual is unable to manage their affairs, a power of attorney can be appointed. While some grant attorneys general powers, others restrict them to specific matters. People with certain disabilities cannot appoint attorneys, and a minor cannot appoint another person to act as their legal representative. In addition, the power of attorneys can be helpful if the borrower cannot sign mortgage documents to transfer or go ahead with a property settlement.

9 Insurance

Before you start to celebrate, you should first arrange insurance because, besides, it being a great idea, most lenders will not release funds until they receive a certificate from the insurer stating that they are the interested party. Overall, protecting your biggest asset is the best thing you can do. too many homeowners are underinsured is often discovered too late. Recent high-profile disasters, such as bush fires, cyclones, or hailstorms, have illustrated just how quickly and people can be left homeless (not to mention out of pocket by thousands of dollars), so getting the right coverage is worthwhile.

Taking out an insurance policy is a common first step when taking out a mortgage. When homeowners have mortgage debt, they focus on what will happen if they cannot repay the debt through death, or if a serious illness reduces their earning capacity. The death of a property owner traumatised families and friends, but how does it they registered the property effect the mortgage?

Those who would benefit from the estate will need to pay off any outstanding mortgages if the property were registered in the sole name of the deceased. The survivor may have difficulty repaying the mortgage because they registered the property as a joint tenancy. Even if the property was sold, the survivor will still have an outstanding mortgage on the property, even though they become the sole owners.

Because the chances of your home being destroyed by fire, or the other natural disaster, is much lower than being robbed, cheaper to insure your actual building than the contents of your home. The responsibility for your new home falls to you on settlement day, so you should make sure that any insurance you take out begins on the day you get the keys and that it is completed before settlement.

Besides the above expenses, consider income protection and insurance for your possessions. Depending on where you live, premiums for contents can be as much as double that of building insurance. You need to balance the likelihood of being robbed or if you live in an area prone to flooding or fires. Pay premiums based on the number of belongings you choose to insure. Once again, you may be tempted to underinsured, but you will have to claim only the amount insured if you are robbed.

10 In Conclusion

To get the ideal plan of action for your property financing needs, our specialists can help you. If you are looking to hire a team of experienced advisers, we are confident that you will want to consider our qualified experts.

If you need information on a wide range of financial products and opportunities, it might be worth contacting a finance broker. A good brokerage has years of experience and will crunch numbers by comparing different loans and recommending a suitable deal for your needs. They interact with lenders on your behalf, and they often attempt to assist after work hours.

Over time, the complexity and requirements of the industry have increased, leading to most charging upfront fees. Many lenders have their criteria for assessing applications, and these are not public knowledge — which can cause some concerns for you when trying to find the right deal. This is where a good finance broker comes in, as they can save you a great deal of time by advising you when to and when not to apply for a loan.

> ▸ Email - support@sherwoodfinance.com.au
>
> ▸ Phone - 1800 743 796

11 Glossary of Terms

Arrangement fees

When lenders charge for the effort of providing financing to a borrower, this fee can vary from one lender to another.

Auction

An auctioneer conducts a sales process in public.

Auctioneer

A profession that oversees the sale of real estate or other items whereby persons become purchasers by competition in public view, the sale favours the highest bidder.

Australian Bureau of Statistics

A federal statutory agency, the Australian Bureau of Statistics (ABS), collects and analyses statistical data and provides evidence-based advice to federal, state and territory governments.

Business activity statements (BAS)

BAS is used to reconciling the tax collected by a business is known as Good and Services Tax (GST), paid to the State government, or annual.

Balance

A statement begins with your last statement's balance, which is the amount you had within your account at the end of the previous report.

Bankruptcy

A legal concept that you would be best to avoid. Also known as Insolvency, this occurs when an individual cannot meet their financial obligations within a reasonable period or if their liabilities exceed their assets.

Bid

A method of purchasing real estate at Auction by an offering.

Caveat

A property caveat is a claim to a property as a legal document. Creating a caveat allows both parties to claim their share of interest. Until the caveat is settled, no further transactions can be registered against the title.

Capital Gains Tax

If you sell an asset such as investment property for a profit, you are subject to capital gains tax (CGT). At the end of the fiscal year, they add the capital gain to your income to be taxed.

Cheque

Cheques detail any amount of money that is withdrawn since account holders often write the cheque to pay someone. This includes the number on the cheque and the amount taken out.

Court judgement

If a person cannot repay their creditors, creditors can get a judgment in court.

Commercial tenants

Commercial, industrial, and retail properties are standard in arranging long-term leases. In addition, outgoings are negotiated but passed onto the tenant.

Commitment fee

A fee is added onto a loan to compensate a lender for their commitment to offering to fund.

Company secretary

A secretary responsibility is to circulate agendas and other documents to directors, shareholders, and auditors and record minutes of shareholder and directors' meetings and resolutions.

Contract of sale

An agreement includes the terms and conditions signed, dated, and witnessed by all related parties.

Conveyance

When real estate is transferred from one party to another, in real estate, this could be when a seller transfers the ownership of a property to a buyer.

Collateral

Collateral is protection to mitigate the risks involved with lending.

Credit

While this refers to several aspects of lending, most used to describe a contract agreement where an individual receives money and repays the lender by a predetermined date (with an added interest fee).

Credit score

Used by lenders to decide whether to accept funding applications based on the risk associated with the borrower. Also referred to as a credit rating.

Development Approval

Local town planning authorities provide written approval of a project, prepared by the developer's or landowner's consultants, allowing the project to move forward as per the development plan.

Deposit

The amount of money needed to be paid upfront as part of the loan agreement. The amount specified can often vary depending on a variety of circumstances.

Division of Property

Fair distribution, or property division, divides property rights and obligations between divorced or De facto spouses and business partners.

Director

An individual manages a company's operations, with the ability to exercise the business' powers for whatever needs it may have.

Economy

A summary of goods, services produced, distributed, and sold within a region or country.

Equity

Property equity is the difference between the remaining debt and the asset's capital value in question.

Exchange of Contracts

When a seller and purchased sign a copy of the sale contract and then exchanges these documents creates a binding agreement for the sale of real estate on agreed terms. The parties are then bound to go ahead to settlement, subject to any cooling-off period that may apply.

First mortgage

When a borrower uses the property as security for the first time as collateral for a loan, as usual, if the mortgage repayments are not met as agreed, the lender can seize the security.

Financial position

An organisation's financial position refers to its assets, liabilities, and equity balances. In a broader sense, the concept can describe the financial condition, which is determined by analysing and comparing its financial statements.

GSA (General Security Agreement)

They register GSA on a National Register to secure the lender's interest against the relevant security entity/asset. As part of the Register, lenders can also negotiate a priority system to make sure that their interests are protected and prioritised.

Guarantor

In property development transactions, lenders could need more security to reduce their risk should the developer default on a loan. This guarantee can take various forms, from cash to property.

Gross Realised Value

In property construction, the Gross Realisation Value is the gross sales (or GST exclusive value of the property) upon the completion of the project. Also known as GRV.

Initial Public Offering

When a company raises capital from public investors by offering shares of a corporation in a public share issuance, often abbreviated to IPO (Initial Public Offering).

Interest rate

The amount of interest charged on a loan, in proportion to the amount borrowed, allows a bank or lender to profit when distributing funds.

Investment property

A real estate purchase intends to earn rental income or capital gain.

Indicative offer

Lenders often show or suggest that the offer may proceed if conditions are met, also known as a conditional offer.

Joint and severally

Where all parties are accountable for the full terms of the agreement, they have entered. For example, in a personal liability case, each party will pursue to repay the entire amount owed.

Land tax

Whether you own or an investment property, you will pay land tax. The amounts vary from state to state.

Lawyer

A lawyer is someone who practices law and deals with legal issues. A lawyer provides legal advice and represents people in court.

Land Banking

Refers to financing secured for the acquisition and holding of developmental sites with no certainty of rapid development.

Legal fees

Upon completing the purchase, the solicitor or conveyancer will charge a fee for the legal work carried out during the purchase process. solicitors charge a flat fee regardless of the property's value.

Letter of Offer

When a lender issues a finance offer to a borrower, it can be accepted or rejected depending on the borrower in question acceptance.

Lease agreements

Lease agreements are made between the property owner and tenant to occupy real estate.

Loan to Value Ratio

All lenders use a Loan to Value Ratio to assess risk when they consider funding and can have a tremendous impact on the terms offered, abbreviated to LTV (loan to values) or LVR (Loan to Value Ratio) (Loan to Value Ratio).

Litigation

When disputes are resolved in court through litigation, unless the parties settle before trial, a judge may make the final decision for the parties in litigation.

Liabilities

Liabilities are obligations between two parties that have not yet been completed or repaid.

Mortgage

A debt passed onto a borrower from a lender secured by a property.

Mortgagee sale

In the event of a default by the mortgagor, the mortgagee claims the security and resells to avoid economic losses.

Mortgagor

A borrower (individual or company) has an interest in a property through a mortgage as security for credit advancement.

Net Realised Value

The asset value realised on the sale is reduced because of standard deductions. so, often abbreviated to NRV.

Non-conforming loans

The term non-conforming loan refers to lending that does not meet the criteria for bank financing.

Non-recourse loan

When a lender can seize the security if a borrower defaults on their payments, the difference from standard scenarios is that the lender cannot get further compensation, even if the collateral covers the total unpaid loan.

Offshore

Ideal for overseas investors, most offshore financing options are available for competitive prices and offer enticing sums of money. The applications to be considered are company borrowers.

Passed in

If the owner's reserve price has not been met, a property is not sold at Auction; therefore, passed in.

Periodic lease

Typical with residential, a tenant continues to rent and occupy the property beyond the expiration of the lease agreement.

Private treaty sale

The terms and conditions of a private sale between a seller and buyer to purchase the real estate vary from state to state.

Presales

A lender will want a certain number of presales to reduce their risks. While the percentage of resold units is not set, funding can vary from one lender to another.

Principal and interest mortgage

A standard mortgage, with the difference that repayments are part capital and part interest.

Property Acquisition

When legal ownership or rights over real estate are transferred, the rules may vary from one state to another.

Property Maintenance

Property owners will need to decide about building works and maintenance. The agent managing your property will manage and looking after the property. This includes marketing your property, collecting rent and fixing any issues.

Progress Payments

As the construction progresses, Lender's drawdown payments in stages. so, the lender needs to report the work completed by its Quantity Surveyor to compare the completed work as part of the loan agreement.

Property Settlement

A legal process facilitated by the legal and financial representatives of the purchaser and the seller. Settlement occurs when ownership is passed from the seller to the buyer. the settlement date is determined in the contract of sale by the vendor.

Profit

When the financial earnings of a business activity exceed the amount needed for the costs, taxes, etc., this could be when a company buys something and sells it for a higher price.

Preferred equity

Investments or loans exceeding the level associated with project and mezzanine debt but not taking part as equal ranking equity are deemed preferred equity.

Rescind

To discontinue a contract of sale.

Reserve Price

The vendor agrees upon the minimum acceptable price before the Auction.

Residential tenants

In most cases, residential leases last for one year; any shorter would be costly for the property owner for re-tenanting costs such as marketing, rental income delays and re-letting fees to the agent.

Recourse

If the debt obligation is not honoured, a lender may seek a borrower's security. A full recourse is when a lender can take more assets to repay the entire unpaid debt.

Receipt

A note any money that is deposited into your account. This is also known as paid-in or credits.

Reserve Bank of Australia

The Australian central bank publishes and controls monetary policy. This can have a varying, underlying effect on mortgage rates.

Settlement Date

The last part of the process is whereby the purchaser completes the payment of the contract price to the seller, and legal possession is transferred to the purchaser.

Share certificates

A share certificate is a document that is issued by a company that sells shares. An investor receives a share certificate upon purchasing a certain number of shares and as a record of ownership.

Stamp duty

All Australian States and Territories impose stamp duty. The amount varies from state to state. Taxes on business purchases differ from taxes on real estate. It arises from the sale or transfer of a wide range of personal and business assets.

Joint tenants

Joint tenancy is the default type of shared ownership. There is no property division between the joint owners; each owns one hundred per cent of the property. Legal ownership of the property passes to the surviving joint owner when a joint owner dies.

Statement of Position

According to their assets and liabilities, companies or individual positions show the current net equity position.

Security

Security on a mortgage is essential because it reduces the risk a lender takes on when providing a loan. Suppose a loan is backed by property, for example. Then, if the borrower defaults on repayments, the lender may seize the property to claim the outstanding debt.

Share certificates

Whenever a company sells shares on the market, it issues shares certificates. As proof of ownership and as a record of the purchase, shares certificates are issued to shareholders.

Shareholders

A person or business that owns a share in a company's stock. They can receive capital gains, take capital losses, and they may receive dividend payments. They are equity owners and have the same benefits and drawbacks as Directors.

Second mortgage

A borrower can offer their real estate as collateral a second time to another lender while the first still has finance secured. As a result, the subsequent lender takes a second charge over the property.

Senior Debt

The registered mortgage holds the property's first ranking for a primary mortgage or principal debt. Developers often prefer senior debt as the margins are lower since banks or significant mortgage funds provide senior debt.

Tax returns

Tax authorities use this process to assess a taxpayer's liability based on their annual income personal circumstances and includes corporate entities.

Tenants in common

A joint ownership arrangement exists when more than one individual owns the same property, but neither has the right of one hundred per cent ownership of the property.

Valuer

A company appointed to conduct the assessment of the current market value of the real estate.

Variation

To change or alter the conditions of the contract of sale.

Valuation

Not to be confused with an appraisal, as a valuation provides a more accurate and recognised property value.

Vendor

In a real estate transaction, a person (s) or entity sells the property.

Quantity Surveyor

A qualified individual that examines costs associated with the building costs. Market conditions impact labour costs and material suppliers with the DA (development approval). Lenders also engage them to make sure that the project is correctly costed.

Yield

An indicator of income by percentage earnt on real estate. It is Calculated by the received net income and the market value of the real estate.

Zoning

The local council planning controls current and future development, including residential, business, and industrial uses.

www.ingramcontent.com/pod-product-compliance
Lightning Source LLC
Chambersburg PA
CBHW041005210326
41597CB00001B/18